THE FREE MIND

EDWARD DE BONO

JAICO PUBLISHING HOUSE

Ahmedabad Bangalore Chennai
Delhi Hyderabad Kolkata Mumbai

Published by Jaico Publishing House
A-2 Jash Chambers, 7-A Sir Phirozshah Mehta Road
Fort, Mumbai - 400 001
jaicopub@jaicobooks.com
www.jaicobooks.com

Published in arrangement with
Phoenix Books
9465 Wilshire Boulevard, Suite 315
Beverly Hills, CA 90212

To be sold only in India, Bangladesh, Bhutan,
Pakistan, Nepal, Sri Lanka and the Maldives.

THE FREE MIND
ISBN 978-81-7992-789-2

First Jaico Impression: 2008
Third Jaico Impression: 2008

Printed by
Trinity Academy For Corporate Training Limited, Mumbai

Foreword

America is the land of the free. The Statue of Liberty is the icon of freedom that greets immigrants who come to America to be more free.

This book is written by someone who believes that too much of the world is unappreciative of the sacrifices made by the USA in the cause of freedom.

In both world wars, the USA came to the rescue of Europe in order to protect its cause. Then the USA intervened in Vietnam, Somalia, Bosnia, and Iraq. Until 9/11 the USA had never been seriously attacked on its home soil.

It is an easy perception to suppose that if a powerful country does something then it must be acting out of its own direct interests.

This is like saying that ultimately all saints are very selfish people. They want to please God and get to heaven. Everything they do is done out of that direct self-interest.

The idealism of the USA may at times be insensitive or even misguided. The way policies are carried through may sometimes be naïve or even clumsy but the effort towards "freedom" is genuine.

There are many conspiracy theories about Iraq and oil supplies. In the end, oil is an international commodity. You sell it on the world market at market prices, or you do not sell it and get no revenue.

It is important that readers of this book should know that I write in admiration of the USA's idealism towards freedom, and the sacrifices made in the name of that idealism.

EDWARD DE BONO

The Road

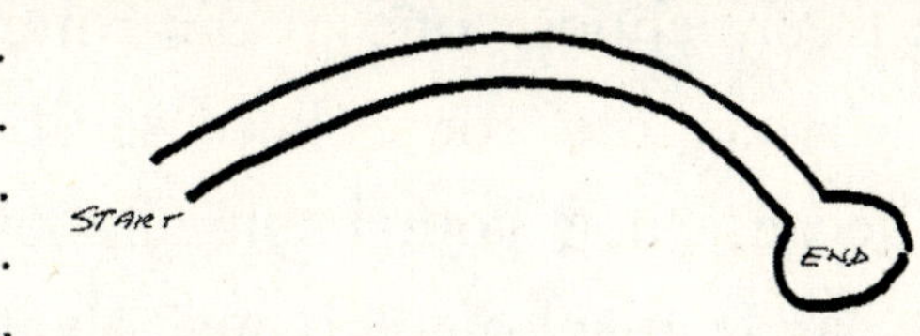

THE ABOVE DIAGRAM SHOWS A SIMPLE and direct road towards a destination. You take that road because it is the only road. You take that road because you want to. You are free to take that road. There is no coercion.

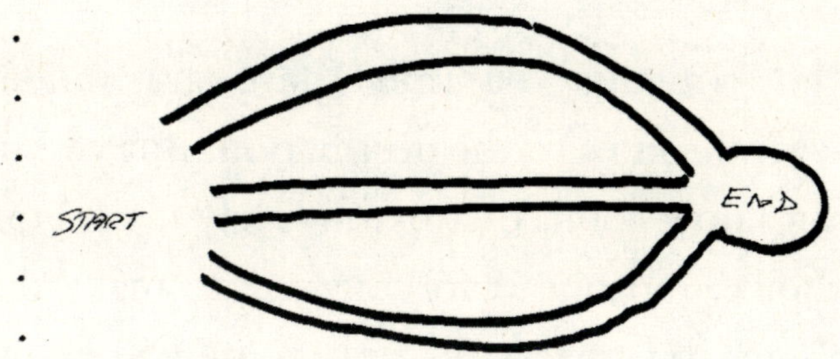

There are now many routes to the destination. You know about the alternative routes. You are free to choose any of the routes.

You freely choose one of the routes. You may choose the route because it is scenic or because it is your habitual route. You have a free choice from several options—and you make your free choice.

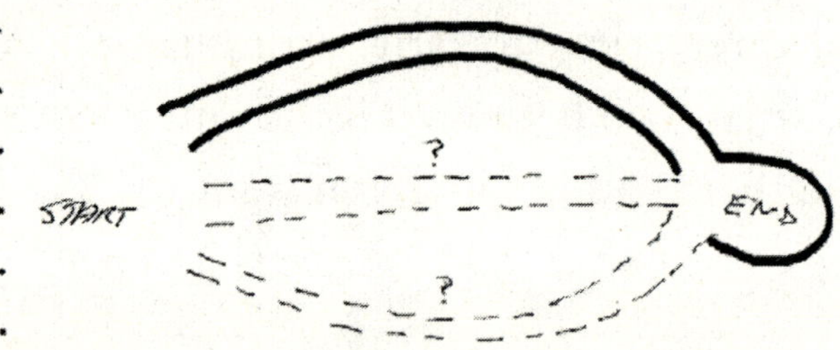

In this diagram there are indeed several routes to the destination. But you do not know about them. You freely make your choice. No one is forcing you to make this choice, but that is the only route you know.

Is this then a truly free choice? There is no coercion, so it must be free.

FREE CHOICES

A MAN IS SITTING AT A TABLE IN A restaurant in France. On the table are a bottle of red wine, a bottle of white wine, a bottle of champagne and a bottle of Budweiser beer. The man is not at all familiar with wine and so he freely chooses the beer. There is no coercion. Is that not a free choice?

I was in Singapore teaching a group of six-year-olds in the excellent School for Thinking set up by Peter and Linda Low to teach my work. I noted that over sixty percent of the youngsters wore spectacles. A lot of Asians do seem to wear spectacles.

I believe that 58% of the Chinese are near-sighted and that this may be due to the shape of their skulls and the length of their eye balls. If spectacles were invented in the 14th century, I began to wonder what the

Chinese did before that. The invention was quite late.

It seems possible that if men were near-sighted and could not wear spectacles (because they had not been invented) then plainer girls had a better chance of getting married. Perhaps that is why there are so many Chinese today?

When I said this to a group of women in China, they said, "You're probably right." When I mentioned it in a seminar in Australia, two women walked out and asked for their money back.

My point is if you cannot see clearly, are you making a free choice? To be sure, no one is forcing you to choose one girl over another. It is a free choice. Or is it?

You could argue exactly the opposite way around. If a man can see very clearly then he can see and choose the prettier girls. Is this free choice? Perhaps it is even less of a free choice. The man is so overwhelmed by physical beauty that he cannot see the personality, temperament, or behavior of the lady in question. So the choice is less free than that of the near-sighted man. Perhaps in those countries where women are so covered up that only the eyes are visible, the choice is more free because the non-visual features are easier to see.

You are planning to go abroad on holiday. The only destinations that you know about are Hawaii and the Caribbean. The only island in the Caribbean that you know about is Puerto Rico. You freely choose Hawaii. No one is forcing you to make that choice. You make it freely. Is it not a free choice?

There is a family tradition that the eldest son be called John. So you choose to call your eldest son John. You have freely chosen to follow the family tradition rather than consider alternatives.

Some Definitions of Freedom

There are many more definitions of freedom than the ones I shall be listing here. The ones I list here are but a sample—a useful sample.

Lack of Coercion

This simply means that you are not "forced" to do something. You are not "forced" to make a certain choice. You are not "forced" to take a certain route. You are free from coercion. You marry the partner you choose. There is no arranged marriage.

Freedom, as the lack of tyranny or force, is the most usual and most used definition. There is a need for such a definition. There is a need to describe a condition that is free from tyranny and oppression.

Free Within a Limited Range of Options

WITHIN AN ARRANGED MARRIAGE YOU may be given the choice of two possible brides. You are free to choose one of them. No one forces your choice. The information on each one is fair and balanced. You have a free choice and you make it.

I once met a very senior Indian business woman who had been educated at Yale and Columbia. She freely chose to go back to India to have her arranged marriage. She told me: "In the West you start with violins in the sunset and then it is downhill all the way to a sixty percent divorce rate. With arranged marriage, you start at the bottom and then invest upwards and make the marriage work."

It was her free choice not to have a free choice.

Almost all our free choices and decisions fall within this definition of "free." We are indeed free within the limited options that are provided by our perceptions, the information we have, and even our expectations.

There are people who go through life bounded by their expectations. They walk past a fashionable (and expensive) restaurant and say to themselves: "That is not for the likes of me." Why not?

Free Within an Unlimited Range of Options

THIS MEANS THAT WE HAVE ALL THE information and a full range of alternative perceptions—then we make our free choice. This is unrealistic since we are never going to have unlimited information. Nor are we going to be able to generate the full range of alternative perceptions. This "full range" of options is so unrealistic that we instantly reject this definition as being impracticable.

This is a mistake. You can travel north even if you are not going to reach the North Pole. You can seek more justice even if you are never going to have perfect justice. So you can seek more information and more options even if you are never going to reach a complete set of options.

The more options you have, the more free your choice, even if you still apply the same values.

Two Definitions

The first definition is the traditional one. Freedom simply means that you are not forced to act in a certain way or to make a certain choice. You are "free" to act as you wish.

The second definition claims that you are not really "free" to choose if you have not really seen the choice.

This book does not deny the validity of the first definition. If you are "forced" to do something you are obviously not free.

But this book sets out to show that you are not really "free" unless you can see before you a wide range of options from which to choose.

Would you go to a used car lot where they had only one car on sale? What sort of free choice would that be?

The more options you open up, the freer your choice.

INFORMATION

IN THE OLD DAYS OF THE COLD WAR there was a story of a race in Moscow. The Russian came second, but the American came in one before the end.

The information omitted that there were only two runners in the race: the American came first and the Russian came last.

Everyone knows about the propaganda used in Nazi Germany and in the former Soviet Union. News and media were strictly controlled and censored. Only certain information could be given out. Even that information was given a specific slant. When needed, stories would be invented to show that the capitalist West was corrupt.

It was not only the media that was controlled. What was taught in school had also to be controlled.

When there is such an obvious control of information it follows that there is little freedom of thinking, freedom of choice or freedom of action.

If your range of information is so obviously limited, you cannot have freedom even if there is no actual coercion to do something.

MEDIA BIAS

THERE IS A STORY THAT WAS ORIGINALLY told about Bill Clinton but is now told about the Italian Prime Minister, Silvio Berlusconi.

One day he was out sailing on his yacht. There was a strong wind and his cap blew off into the sea. He got out of the boat and walked across the top of the water to retrieve his cap. He returned to the boat and said: "You see the newspapers tomorrow. They will say that Signor Berlusconi cannot even swim."

Even if there is no control or censorship at all, information is severely restricted by the natural, and logical, behavior of the media.

Interest

The media has a commercial obligation—and a responsibility to its shareholders—to sell newspaper copies. To do this, the content of the media has to be of interest.

Experience has shown that readers or viewers are more interested in the negative, the unusual or the bizarre. Some time ago, in Germany, someone advertised on the internet for someone "who wanted to be eaten." Someone replied to the advertisement and was indeed killed and eaten. For a long time, this filled newspaper columns around the world.

Scandals are interesting. In some countries sex scandals are a sure source of interest. The stories can run and run. Someone who has done excellent work becomes known only for some trivial sex scandal.

Bill Clinton's presidency will be forever marred by the international media coverage of his affair with 22-year-old intern, Monica Lewinski.

When Anna Nicole Smith died, all other US news ceased to exist. The whole of the country was transfixed by: her enormous breast implants; her marriage to an 89-year-old octogenarian, 63 years her senior; her 10-year court battle for his fortune; the sudden death of her teenage son; and her "commitment ceremony" to long-time attorney, Howard K. Stern. Her tragic end only served to peak the media's attention and, without exception, every news outlet cashed in on her death. The coverage that Anna Nicole Smith received was a media phenomenon because her story continued to attract the public's attention for months on end, and the media continued to sell it to them.

Being captivated by scandal is the essence of human interest. I would even go so far as to suggest taxing newspapers (half the advertising rate for the same space), which sell political, financial, or sexual misconduct in order to increase their profits.

NEGATIVITY

THE NEGATIVE POINTS ABOUT A political candidate are seen to be more interesting than the positive points. Political campaigning seeks to focus on the negative.

A bridge that falls down is more newsworthy than the building of a new bridge.

Interviews tend to be more negative than positive. This is because it is much more difficult to make positive features as interesting. Also it is assumed, in some countries like the UK, that the reader will always be jealous of success and will want to find something negative about a successful person. To be fair, this is not so much the case in the USA, which may possibly be the only country in the world where success is honored rather than envied.

Selectivity

This is inevitable. It would not be possible to include all aspects of a story. Some things are going to be left out. What is left out depends on the point of view of the journalist or the editor. Usually the intention of the journalist is to tell a certain story and what fits with that story is included and what does not fit is excluded.

Dishonesty

Occasionally, the media is blatantly dishonest. In the pursuit of a story truth becomes irrelevant. I have had a few personal experiences with that in the UK.

In the UK fifty-six percent of youngsters believe newspapers to be dishonest. This view at an early age should be concerning.

Not Deliberate

I do not want to give the impression that the media is deliberately biased—though this may occasionally be the case. It is just that the very nature of the media, and of assumed readers' and viewers' interest, leads to inevitable information that is not completely accurate.

A Simple Test

There is quite a simple way to test the completeness of your information. For example, in a political campaign you ask yourself to list all the good points about the candidate you are not going to vote for. So if you feel you are going to vote Democrat you forcc yourself to list the good points about the Republican candidate and the other way around. It is not at all easy to do. This test is a little unfair on the media because your selective perception may have picked out certain points and ignored others which were indeed reported.

Perception

Everyone knows about the importance of information. Few people know about the huge importance of perception.

Perception is real even when it is not reality.

David Perkins at Harvard did some research which showed that ninety percent of the errors in thinking were errors of perception—not logic. This fits in with my own experience.

Traditionally, education has put all the emphasis on logic. In real life thinking, logic plays a relatively minor part compared to perception.

If your perception is faulty then your answer will be rubbish even if your logic is perfect.

Goedel's theorem showed that from within a system you could never logically prove its starting points. Perception is the starting point of thinking.

Not long ago, I was attending an economics advisory board meeting. After the meeting in Australia one of the participants came up to me and said: "I read one of your books as a young man that changed my thinking, and as a result I won the Nobel Prize [in medicine]." That book was all about the importance of perception.

In Australia, the one-dollar coin is much bigger than the two-dollar coin. One day, his friend offered five-year-old Johnny a choice between two coins: a one-dollar coin and the small two-dollar coin. He could take and keep whichever one he wanted. He picked the bigger, one-dollar coin. His friends laughed and giggled.

Whenever they wanted to tease Johnny they offered him again this choice of coins. He always took the bigger one. He never seemed to learn.

One day an adult saw this and called Johnny over. He told Johnny that although the smaller coin was smaller it was actually worth more. "I know that," said Johnny, "But how often would they have offered me the coins if I had taken the smaller one the first time?"

A perception that looked at the choice at one point in time would have led to the selection of the smaller, two-dollar coin. A perception that looked ahead over time would have seen the possibility of many one-dollar coins.

A man of sixty-five got a glamorous young girlfriend of twenty by lying about his age. He told the girl he was ninety-five!

An old man of ninety goes down to Hell. As he wanders around he sees a friend of his, about the same age, with the most beautiful young woman on his knee.

He asks, “Is this hell? You seem to be having a good time.”

The friend replies, “It is indeed Hell. I am the punishment for the young lady.”

The essence of humor is the change of perception to an unexpected one which is perfectly logical once the change has been made.

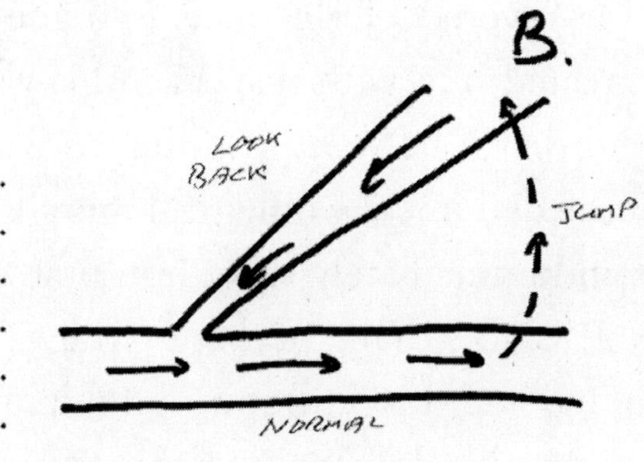

In the diagram we go along the usual road. Suddenly we are taken to the end of the side road (B). Once there we look back and find it to be a perfectly logical position.

This behavior is inevitable in any self-organizing information system like the human brain. Once we can understand this behavior we can develop the formal tools of "lateral thinking." These are deliberate tools for generating ideas. They can be powerful. Using just one of the tools, a group of workshops in South Africa generated 21,000 ideas for a steel company in one afternoon.

A revered cleric once told me how they treated him with respect in his village. He said that if he went into the store and it was crowded they would call him to the front and immediately serve him first.

I said that perhaps they were gossiping and his entrance inhibited that gossip. Maybe they wanted to get him out quickly in order to resume the gossip.

The Problem with Perception

The problem with perception is that there may be many alternative perceptions, alternative ways of looking at something. The problem is also that you cannot logically derive all these possible perceptions.

We need to develop the skill of "perpetual thinking" which is very different from logical thinking. We need to develop the skill of possibility thinking.

Possibility

Two thousand years ago, China was far ahead of the West in science and technology. They had gunpowder, rockets, etc. Had China continued at the same rate of development, today China would easily be the dominant power in the world—in science, technology, commerce, military power, etc. They are highly intelligent and very hard working people. So what went wrong?

The scholars started to believe you could move from "certainty" to "certainty" to "certainty." They did not like the uncertainty and messiness of possibility. As a result they never developed the "possibility" system. They never developed speculation, hypothesis, guesses, etc. So progress came to a dead end.

If I had been alive in China in the year 900, and if they had listened to me, then China would be the dominant power in the world today.

Interestingly, the same thing is happening in the West today. Computers mean that information can be collected, stored and analyzed.

People are starting to realize that information is all we need. That information will do our thinking for us. Scientists are starting to believe that analyzing data is all that is needed.

Some time ago a senior officer in the French government research organization (CNRS) came to see me and asked if I could help his scientists generate hypotheses—and therefore alternatives and possibilities. He told me they believed that analysis of data was enough.

In my experience at some major universities such as Oxford, Cambridge, London, and Harvard, I have to say that the time spent on possibility and hypothesis was totally insufficient.

Source of Perceptions

PERCEPTIONS ARE WAYS OF ORGANIZING the world around. They are a way of organizing the information we see or hear around us.

A few perceptions come from personal experience. The majority come from tradition, education, family influences, etc. These are ready-made perceptions.

Human language is by far the biggest barrier to human progress. Language is an encyclopedia of ignorance. Words entered language at a relative stage of ignorance and became frozen into performance. These words now force us to perceive the world in a very old-fashioned way.

For example we have the perception that political parties are like tribes or clans. You belong to one or the other and the other tribe is a sort of "enemy."

How often do you hear someone say: "In my life about half the time I have voted Democrat and the other half I have voted Republican"?

If someone did say this you would suppose that the person used to vote one way and then "saw the light" and changed. You would not imagine that the person sometimes voted one way and sometimes the other depending on the policies and personalities on offer.

We very rarely challenge our perceptions. This is never a matter of seeking to prove that a perception is wrong. This would be very difficult. It is more a matter of generating other possibilities, of generating other perceptions so that we are no longer so rigidly certain of our initial perception.

Selective Perceptions

If you saw the film Fahrenheit 9/11 you would have seen how effective selective perception can be. Once you have an overall perception on a specific issue, you only see those things that support this perception—and you put them into a very well-made film.

Once our perceptions are formed, we see the world through those perceptions. We only see those things that support our perception and ignore what does not. It is not that we reject those things that do not support our perception; we simply do not notice or see them at all.

Perceptions and Freedom

Our range of options is severely restricted by our limited perceptions. If we can only see things in one way then we are not free to choose between options.

We need to develop perceptual skill and the skill of "possibilities." How we might do this is considered later in this book.

Perception is a very, very important part of thinking, freedom and choice.

It is interesting that no religion has explicitly emphasized humor. Yet humor is a key lubricant of life. Humor is the best anti-despair and anti-arrogance device we have. Humor urges us to look at things in a different way. Humor is about the possibility of perceptual change.

PROTEST

THERE IS A FIRE AND A FIRE ENGINE hurries to the scene to put the fire out.

A group of protesters object that the fire engine is blocking the road. They cannot get to work. They cannot go shopping. They cannot take the kids to school.

Soon another group of protesters gather to protest at the huge waste of water. They point out that there are millions of people around the world who are severely short of water. Right here, water is being used lavishly.

When the fire is out, a further group of protesters object to the mess. There is all that black stuff about, it spoils the washing on the line, pets bring the black stuff into the house, etc.

Finally there is another group of protesters who want to know why the fire engine took so long to arrive and why the equipment used was not the very latest.

Someone even suggests an inquiry into how the fire started in the first place. Were safety regulations breached?

Protest is an essential part of a free and democratic society. Protest is the direct way that the conscience of society can be expressed in between elections.

But protest can be selective. In the above example, the fact that the fire was put out and did not spread to adjacent buildings was ignored or "taken for granted" (that is what a fire service is for).

I was once told by a senior union leader that the more successful the union was in fighting for the rights of workers, the less the workers wanted to join the union.

"You are fighting for us. We will get the benefits. Why should we bother to join?"

I told this story to a senior French diplomat just before the Iraq war. He got very upset and asked whether I was suggesting that France was standing back, but would get the benefits of the US invasion of Iraq.

In the days of the Soviet Union I was invited to Moscow by the Academy of Science to talk to the Pedagogy section, the Psychology section, and the Philosophy section. They were interested in teaching my thinking methods across all schools.

They told me that the only mental activity open to mentally energetic youngsters was to be against everything. That was the easiest thinking. If youngsters could be taught to think constructively that could change.

At a meeting of the Foreign Affairs Committee of Politburo, in the Kremlin, the chairman had my book on Conflict Resolution in front of him. There were many notes in the margin. He saw me looking at it and said:

"This is not Gorbachev's copy. He has his own."

I was later told by a senior politician from Kazakhstan that in the days of

Perestroika, my books were top reading in the Kremlin.

Constructive and creative thinking are as important as protest.

Protest is really a vote of confidence in the authorities. There is confidence that if something is complained about then the authorities have the skill to put it right. Sometimes this confidence is misplaced.

Protest is important. But it is not the most constructive aspect of human thinking. The idiom of protest arises from our traditional and very restricted view of human thinking as expressed in critical thinking (from the Greek "Kritikos" for judge). This matter will be explored later.

Design

More information can provide the additional options that may make you fully free.

Changes in perceptions may also provide those additional options.

The third source of further options is "design."

You can analyze the past but you have to design the future.

We have been so obsessed with analysis that we have neglected design. We think of design only in terms of clothes, wallpaper or a new car.

Western thinking was originated by the Greek "Gang of Three" (GG3).

There was Socrates who was obsessed with Argument. He has a reputation for asking questions, but he actually asked mostly leading questions.

There was Plato with his search for Truth and his disdain for democracy.

There was Aristotle with his "box"-type Logic. According to him, there were category boxes. You judged something into a box and then you read the label on the box.

At the Renaissance this thinking was introduced into Europe by the Arabs in

Spain. Education at that time was mainly in the hands of Church people. They did not need design thinking, or creative thinking, or perceptual thinking. What was needed was the search for the "truth" and the argument needed to prove heretics wrong. That became Western thinking and remains so to this day.

A child with a rash is brought to a doctor's clinic. The doctor examines the child, asks some questions and does some tests. What is this? The doctor makes a judgment or diagnosis. This involves putting the condition into a defined box—say measles. Once this judgment has been made, the doctor knows all about the condition from the accumulated wisdom of other doctors and research about measles. The doctor knows the probable course of the illness, the possible complications and the standard treatment.

That is the model for almost all our thinking. Analyze the situation and identify standard elements. Then apply the standard responses to these standard elements. One hundred percent of education is about that. Ninety percent of our daily thinking is like that.

Alan Greenspan in the Federal Reserve Bank in Washington looks at the economic situation. If he identifies this as "inflation" then the standard answer is to raise interest rates. If he identifies it as recession then the standard answer is to lower interest rates—which for various reasons does not work too well.

Is there anything wrong with this sort of thinking? No, it is excellent and very powerful.

Is there anything wrong with the front left wheel of a motor car? No, it is excellent and essential.

But if you believed that all you needed on a motor car was the front left wheel there would be something seriously wrong with your belief.

If you believe that analysis and judgment thinking are enough there is something seriously wrong with this belief.

At the Renaissance the Church was obsessed with the "truth." The purpose of thinking was to find and defend the truth.

You are driving along a road and the car runs out of gas. You get out and declare that you have reached your "destination." When we have run out of "thinking" we declare that we have reached the "truth."

Design is putting together the ingredients we have in order to reach the values we want.

In my book, *WHY SO STUPID? How the Human Race has never really learned to Think* (see appendix) I explore this point in much more detail.

Discovery is Not Enough

It is not just a matter of discovering alternatives and options. These may be waiting to be discovered. That is not enough. We need to "design" options that have never existed before.

This is why I set up "The World Centre for New Thinking" (see appendix) to design the options that representative bodies, like the UN and democracies, cannot put forward. By definition a new idea is new and not representative of current thinking. So any really new idea is high risk for representative bodies. But once put forward an idea cannot be unthought-of. So there is a need for a platform to make new ideas visible and to organize task forces to generate new ideas on specific issues.

Options have to be designed as well as discovered. You can only have truth about the past. About the future you can only have "possible value."

We need to learn the habits and skills of design thinking. We need to give "design" a much more prominent place in our thinking. Analysis and judgment are not enough.

The education system is not doing enough if it simply teaches the standard responses and analysis as a way of identifying standard situations.

Human Software

We all know about computer software. There are thousands of people all over the world writing software for computers. Bill Gates and others have become deservedly rich writing and organizing computer software.

What about human software? In the end human software is far more important and far more fundamental than computer software.

For centuries we have been satisfied with human software that is powerful but limited.

Our analysis and judgment system has been excellent in science and technology. If you identify a material as "iron" then you know all about it and its behavior. All this is predictable. You put iron together with something else and you get technology.

Sadly, this thinking has been almost useless in human affairs where we have made little progress. People are not as predictable as "iron." Furthermore there are "loops." If you call someone an "idiot" that person changes and is no longer the same person you called an idiot.

We need design thinking.

Take one aspect of human thinking. This is our revered "argument" system that we use in government and in the courts of law. It is an incredibly crude, primitive and ineffective system.

In a court of law, if the prosecuting attorney thinks of a point that is going to favor the defense, does that lawyer put it forward? Of course not. If the defense attorney thinks of a point that will help the prosecution, is that point put forward? Of course not. This is "case making" rather than exploration of the subject.

All the effort goes into proving that something is "A" or "not A" (or "B"). No effort goes into designing "C," "D," or other possibilities.

In the adversarial argument system there are emotions of "win/lose" and "attack/defend." Egos are involved and affect the outcome.

With the argument you have to take the "position" right at the beginning. You hope—not very sincerely—that your position will be modified in the course of the argument.

With true "exploration" of a subject you explore the subject first and then come to a position right at the end.

But what could we use instead of argument?

Imagine four people each facing one side of a building. Through a walkie-talkie system they are arguing as to which is the most beautiful side of the building.

It is suggested that they walk around so that at each moment all of them are looking at the same side.

"Parallel thinking" means that at any moment everyone is looking and thinking in the same direction. There is no attack and defense.

This is a system that I designed many years ago and it is now widely in use in classrooms and corporations around the world. There are six modes of thinking. Each mode is symbolized by a colored "hat." So when the Black Hat is in use everyone is focusing on possible dangers, critical points, weaknesses, faults, etc. When the Yellow Hat is in use everyone focuses on the benefits and values. The Green Hat is for creativity and new ideas. The Red Hat is permission to put forward emotions, intuition and feelings—without any need to justify them. The Blue Hat is the organizing Hat. The White Hat is a focus on information.

The system is in use with four-year-olds and with senior executives at some of the world's largest corporations.

ABB in Finland reported that they used to spend thirty days on their multi-national project discussions. Using the hats they do it in two days. MDS, a medium sized corporation in Canada, reported that they had saved $20 million the first year they used the Hats. I was recently told by a Nobel Prize-winning economist that at a top economics meeting, those taking part were using the Hats.

Suppose someone is against an idea being discussed. Normally, that person would use every moment and every bit of intellectual energy to point out the faults in the idea. With the Hat system, that person would be fully encouraged to be cautious under the Black Hat. But when the Yellow Hat came around that person would be expected to find values. If that person was unable to find values while everyone else did find values then that person would be seen by everyone to be "stupid." If the values are there, why can you not see them?

Everyone is challenged to use their thinking fully to explore the subject—not to make a case.

Statoil in Norway had a problem with an oil rig. The problem was costing them $100,000 a day. They had been thinking about it for some time. Then Jens Arup, who is trained in these methods, introduced parallel thinking. In twelve minutes they had a solution which saved $10 million. In the USA, Grant Todd has been investigating the use of parallel thinking with juries, which has produced some powerful results—unanimous decisions were reached very quickly. Instead of adversarial argument the jury fully explores the evidence and comes to a joint conclusion.

Parallel Thinking (the Six Hats) is only one example of the human software that has been designed and tried out. "Lateral

Thinking" provides formal tools for deliberate creativity. There are other types of software which will be mentioned later.

We are not free if we are told what to think. We are only free if we are taught to think. Judgment and critical thinking are never enough because they lack the generative, creative design elements of thinking.

FREE TO THINK?

IF YOU ARE FREE TO THINK, ARE YOU free to think?

No.

I was being taken around a famous pottery workshop. I was told that I was free to make any design I wanted. I was free to create any shape.

Was I free?

I was not being forced to do any specific shape. I was free to make what I wanted.

There was no force or coercion, but was I free?

Since I had very little idea about handling the clay and making pottery items, I was only free in theory. I was free to do anything. But I did not know how to make anything.

You may be free to think. There may be no coercion at all. You are not forced to think one way or another. But if you do not know how to think, are you really free to think? You are no more free than I was in that pottery workshop. Now, if someone had shown me how to make pottery (which they offered to do) I would have been free to make anything.

If you are not free to think up options and alternatives you are not free to decide between them. And you are not really free to think up options and alternatives unless you have been taught how to think.

Unfortunately, that is not the case in the USA, or almost everywhere else.

IS INTELLIGENCE ENOUGH?

THERE IS A WIDESPREAD BELIEF THAT if you are intelligent you are a good thinker and if you are not so intelligent you are not such a good thinker.

This is complete, and dangerous, rubbish.

Many highly intelligent people fall into the "intelligence trap." There are many aspects to this.

An intelligent person takes a view on a subject and then uses his, or her, intelligence to defend that view. The more intelligent the person the better the defense is of that view. The better the defense of the view the less there is any need to listen to anyone else or to look for alternatives. If you are "right" and you know you are "right" why listen to anyone else?

So, highly intelligent people can get locked into a view simply because they can defend it so well. This is very poor thinking. Defending a view is not a great intellectual feat.

If you choose your starting perceptions and starting values, you can defend almost any point of view.

Intelligent people grow up knowing that they are rather more intelligent than those around them. So they want to get the most immediate gratification through proving other people wrong. This is sensible because proving someone wrong is immediate and rewarding. Making a constructive suggestion is delayed and uncertain.

Intelligent people can quickly scan the information and lock into a standard response. Less intelligent people cannot do this and may have to think longer and may, occasionally, come up with a different response.

Intelligence is like the horse-power of a car. Thinking is like the skill with which the car is driven. You may have a very powerful car driven badly. You may have a more humble car driven more skillfully.

We waste high intelligence unless we explicitly teach thinking skills. We certainly waste lesser intelligence unless we explicitly teach thinking skills.

I was once asked to teach thinking to a group of Nobel Prize winners. At first they implied, very politely, that no one could teach them thinking because, after all, they had shown their thinking skill in winning the Nobel Prize. At the end of three days they went away saying: "Yes, these do work."

I have talked at meetings of Nobel Prize winners on several occasions. Within their own fields they are brilliant. But if you ask a Nobel Prize winner in physics to have ideas on dealing with traffic congestion in cities, the thinking is certainly good but not exceptional. They seem to have built up a skill handling the idioms within specific fields—rather than a generalized skill of thinking that could be applied to any subject.

Intelligence is possibly determined by the speed of transmission along the neurons in the brain. It is an ability to understand and comprehend but not necessarily an ability to "design a way forward." Understanding and recognizing are not the same as design and creativity.

If "thinking" is needing a skill and not just a matter of intelligence, what can we do about it?

Thinking and School

John Edwards, in Australia, showed that if you taught less science, but some thinking to science students, they did better in the science exams.

He also showed that in a school where twenty-six percent of students reached the top level in mathematics, teaching thinking increased this to fifty percent, even though no extra mathematics was taught at all.

There are many schools in the UK which have shown that teaching thinking greatly improves the performance in standard examinations in other subjects.

Three Standard Myths

There are three standard and rather rigid myths in education. These myths are perpetuated not out of dogmatic rigidity but more out of ignorance: "They know not what they do."

The First Myth

The first myth is that if someone is indeed thinking, then that person is learning to think. If that were true there would be a lot of genius lawyers around.

In any skill you establish a basic "get by" habit. As you practice the skill you practice this habit more and more.

If you develop the skill of being a poor thinker you will in time become an "excellent poor thinker."

It is also assumed that as you learn the traditional subjects (geography, history, science, etc.) you will develop skill thinking. This is partly true. You will develop skills of data analysis, understanding and judgment. But you will not develop any skills of the "design group": perceptual thinking; constructive thinking; design thinking; and creative thinking. Analysis, judgment and logic are simply not enough.

THE SECOND MYTH

THIS IS THE HOPE, AND BELIEF, THAT if you teach standard subjects in a "thinking way" then you will be teaching thinking.

So if you encourage students to ask questions and to challenge assumptions, this will develop thinking skills. It does. But the thinking is very limited to data analysis and leaves out the productive, generative and constructive aspects of thinking.

The "scholarship" mode so beloved of universities is highly dangerous. At the time of the Renaissance, universities realized that there was a great deal to learn from the past, especially from the Greek thinkers including both the Gang of Three and the pre-Socratic thinkers (who were actually better thinkers). So scholarship became a key idiom of universities.

The value of scholarship is that it makes life easier both for teacher and students. The teacher can just ask the students to look up texts. The students need only to only access texts and analyze them.

The teaching of Psychology just becomes the History of Psychology.

Harvard prides itself on scholarship. When I was teaching at Harvard (medical faculty) I found it much more useful to work with people at MIT who were more into "design."

Harvard Business School prides itself on the analysis of "case studies." When I was an examiner in the medical school at Cambridge University, I came to realize the limitations of case studies in medicine. They are good for motivation but not much good for teaching basic principles.

I am told that a lot of brilliant people come out of Harvard Business School. I am sure that is so. If a lot of brilliant people walk under an archway then a lot of brilliant people will come out of the archway—which may have contributed very little. You have to be brilliant to get into the Business School, so you will be brilliant when you come out of it.

I am not implying that this emphasis on analysis and scholarship is worthless. I accept the great value of analysis. The danger is when we come to believe that this is all there is to "thinking" and we leave out the very important "design group" elements.

The Third Myth

This is the belief that teaching "critical thinking" is teaching thinking. Clearly it is teaching thinking in the sense that it is not teaching the making of donuts!

Imagine six brilliantly trained critical thinkers sitting around a table to discuss a new project. None of them can get going until someone suggests a "design" for the project.

As I mentioned before, the word "critical" comes from the Greek word for "judge" (kritikos). Judgment thinking is very valuable and stops us from doing things that are wrong, dangerous or ineffective. But it is not enough.

The huge problem with education over the centuries has been this myth that judgment thinking is enough. It derives from the Gang of Three (GG3) thinking and from the Church needs of the Renaissance.

Sometimes it is suggested that "critical" really means "very important" as we might talk about a "critical decision." This is misleading and sometime dishonest.

We do need a word for "judgment thinking" and that word is "critical thinking." To pretend that this word covers all aspects of thinking is dangerous and deceptive.

THE BASIC MYTH

THE MOST BASIC, AND INNOCENT, belief is that thinking cannot be taught. It is assumed that it is just a matter of intelligence. It is assumed that if you just point out the mistakes in thinking and in logic, that is the best you can do.

This myth is directly based on innocence and ignorance. Most educators do not know how thinking can be taught. Most educators have not seen the powerful and simple ways in which thinking can be taught. Most educators have not seen the effect on students of teaching thinking directly and explicitly.

Children love thinking. At a school in the UK, the main punishment for wrongdoing of any sort was non-admittance into the student's thinking lessons. Every idea is an achievement for a student.

A student may not be good at standard subjects and have a low self-esteem as a result. That student may not be good at the traditional academic game of "guessing what the teacher wants." In the thinking lessons, the student realizes that he or she can indeed think and come up with ideas.

Teachers often react with surprise: "I always thought Susan was rather slow, but in the thinking lessons she showed she was not slow at all."

"I thought Johnny was stupid and so did most classmates. But in the thinking lessons he came up with good ideas that no one else had thought of."

In Bulgaria (in the Marxist days) they started to use my work in schools and did follow-up research. They asked a nine-year-old from Plovdiv (the second city in Bulgaria) if she used the methods she learned in the thinking class in "real life."

She replied: "I use these things all the time in real life. I even use them outside life—in school."

What Can Be Done

So what can be done to make Americans more truly free?

Observation, comment, analysis and complaint are not enough. What can be suggested? What can be done?

What are the possible ways forward?

I have never felt it to be my business to "persuade" anyone to do something. That requires salesmanship skills at which I am not especially good.

I simply want to point out possibilities. The possibilities are there to be made into realities.

I also want to point out that there is a huge amount of experience with the methods that will be suggested. The experience is with different abilities, different age groups, different cultures, different religions, etc. From Down syndrome youngsters to top executives; from aboriginals in Australia to Nobel Prize laureates; from elementary schools to universities, the experience is there.

One educator once wrote: "These things are so simple that they cannot really work." That is rather like claiming that "cheese does not exist." Cheese does exist. The methods do work. In practical terms what matters is "powerful simplicity." Complicated philosophical analysis may have no operating value. Practical tools are needed.

The (Possible) Way Forward

Laying out a route does not mean that you have to take that route. The route becomes an option, an alternative and a possibility. You are free to choose not to take the route. In that choice you are more free than if you had not become aware of the option.

There are four areas of possible activity:

1. Education

This largely concerns schools but also includes other educational institutes such as universities, technical colleges, etc.

2. Home

This focuses on the family and what you can do at home. Do you have to wait until the local school teaches thinking? If your youngster seems to be undervalued by the school, what can you do at home?

3. Individual

This is your choice as an individual. What can you do? What actions and options are open to you?

4. Organizations

This includes business corporations, government bodies and any other organizations. There is quite a lot of activity in this section because business has always shown more interest in "thinking" than any other sector of society.

Each of these sections will be considered separately. There will be an overlap between the sections.

The role of a doctor is a diagnosis followed by treatment. My background as a physician suggests that diagnosis without treatment is not enough.

Extortion is not enough. For example, exhorting people to be creative sounds good at the time, but the effect wears off in less than a week. There have to be practical tools that can be learned and used into the future.

Detailed information on the various items and courses, etc. can be found in the appendix.

EDUCATION

YEARS OF EXPERIENCE ACROSS A WIDE range of abilities, ages and cultures have shown that it is possible to teach "thinking" explicitly as a subject in its own right.

This thinking is not the old-fashioned notion of syllogisms and logical progression but "real life" thinking.

Critical thinking does indeed have a role, but by itself it is totally insufficient since it lacks the productive or "design group" aspects of thinking (perceptual, constructive, creative and design thinking). Any claim to cover all these simply makes nonsense of the term "critical" and is dangerously dishonest.

I believe that every school from the earliest age onward should spend a minimum of two periods a week on "thinking" as a subject. For many years this has been the case in Venezuela where I had been invited by Luis Alberto Machado (Minister of State for the Development of Intelligence) to develop "thinking" as a subject.

What should be taught? Most important of all is the teaching of "perception." Nothing is more important than this because if your perception is inadequate nothing else matters. For the teaching of perception there is the CoRT (Cognitive Research Trust) program which I shall describe later.

In addition, there is a need for the Six Hats method of parallel thinking from the earliest school age. This develops the skill of using your mind fully rather than just taking a position and defending it.

Elements of "lateral thinking" can also be taught to teach "idea creativity."

There is other material that can be added to these basics. It is, however, important to keep in mind that if whisky and gin are excellent drinks, then a mixture of whisky and gin is not twice as excellent but awful. So mixing in different approaches, each of which is excellent, may be confusing and useless.

Later on, it would be helpful to teach some "design thinking" directly in a practical way. It would also be helpful to teach some "business thinking" and how value is created in society. Usually the closest contact youngsters have with business thinking is the game of Monopoly, which is based on the business strategy: "I got here first so you have to pay me rent" (no productive effort at all).

Some universities around the world have started to introduce my work on thinking as part of a foundation course. This makes sense. The University of Pretoria (the largest in Africa with ninety thousand students) is one of them.

I am often told that curriculum is full and that there is simply no space to introduce thinking. If you say this slowly, it must be the most shocking statement ever uttered about education:

"Our curriculum is so full that we do not have time to teach 'thinking.'"

Thinking is the most fundamental of all skills—and more important than almost anything else.

Nevertheless, this is a practical statement. The answer is to make space. If you cannot do this, then introduce thinking as part of English Language. Research shows, repeatedly, that better thinking has more effect on writing than anything else.

In one small study, seven-year-olds were asked to write on a subject. They wrote an average of four lines. After they had been taught the Six Hats, they wrote forty lines.

In some countries the thinking lessons are used as a method for teaching English. The urge to express your thoughts is more powerful than the urge to describe "your holidays."

I am very often asked whether "thinking" should be taught explicitly as a separate subject or infused into all subject areas.

The answer is very clear. "Thinking" needs to be taught explicitly as a separate subject. This way a youngster develops an explicit skill and confidence in thinking, even if he or she is poor at other subjects. Once thinking is taught explicitly and separately as a subject then it can be infused into all subject areas—and should be.

The European Union spends about twenty-five percent of school time on mathematics. Most people use three percent of the mathematics they learn at school. It is said the rest is there to "train the mind." If that is so, then it makes sense to teach thinking directly and explicitly. Playing chess possibly trains the mind, but, judging by the personal lives of some great chess players, suggests that this thinking does not carry over into real life.

Home

If the local school does not teach thinking, what can you do?

If you feel that your child is undervalued by the local school, because he, or she, does not excel at academic work, what can you do? You can set out to teach thinking at home. You do not have to wait for your school to catch up.

I am setting up a "home thinking network." One evening a week is designated as the "thinking evening." That evening the family, and possibly neighbors, meets to enjoy thinking as a hobby. Each week there will be new material: new lessons and new exercises. Thinking can be made as enjoyable as sport—and with a greater sense of achievement.

There is also a book I wrote many years ago with the title, "Teach Your Child How to Think."

From time to time, small thinking exercises and the use of "thinking tools," can be introduced into conversation, while driving, at meals, etc.

Youngsters love thinking. The sculptor Rodin did a great disservice to thinking by showing the thinker as a solemn fellow with a heavy head resting on his hand. Thinking can be fun. What would happen if dogs could be taught to speak? Youngsters enjoy thinking through the consequences of such a suggestion.

Individual

What can you do as an individual?

There are many books to read, mine included.

You can set up a "thinking club" and run things along the lines of the Home Thinking Network, using the same material and methods.

I also intend to set up some internet courses directly organized by myself. It is important to be sure that any such course is directly organized and authorized by myself as there are many who claim they are running courses with my material.

ORGANIZATIONS

OVER THE YEARS, MANY WELL KNOWN organizations, have sought instruction in my methods of thinking such as IBM, Shell, Prudential, GM, Ford, Bank of America, etc.

When I wrote my first book on thinking, businesses immediately showed interest. In my experience, business has shown more interest in thinking than any other sector of society. This is because there is "bottom line" reality. You need to do things. You need to make things happen. If you do not show profits, shareholders are going to get upset. In other sectors, such as politics or the academic world, it is enough to convince people that you are right, verbally; you do not need to show results. There are over twelve hundred certified trainers in my work around the world. Some are independent and some are within corporations. For example, Siemens, the largest corporation in Europe, had thirty-seven internal trainers.

The network is organized by APTT (Advance Practical Thinking Training) out of Des Moines, Iowa.

In Singapore, Peter and Linda Low are probably the most successful trainers in the world. They have trained over thirty thousand executives in small groups. They also run a Saturday "thinking school" for youngsters. There is always a need for more trainers.

The most requested program is the parallel thinking of the Six Hats. This is seen to save a huge amount of money (millions of dollars) and time. It is seen to be constructive rather than destructive. It challenges people to use all their thinking to explore a subject rather than just take up an "argument position."

I was once told that J.P. Morgan in Europe had reduced their meeting time to one fifth of what it had been. I was also told that a top IBM research laboratory had reduced the meeting time to one quarter.

Under the guidance of David Turner, DuPont was a big user of these methods, and ended up with some powerful results.

How Can Thinking Be Taught?

Most educators, and other people, simply do not know that thinking can be taught directly. Our traditions of education are very old-fashioned. They go back to the days when some people could read and write and think and others did as they were told. We do not realize just how "feudal" the idioms in education are. Thinking was not for the serfs.

Those who have tried out the methods mentioned here find them to be simple, powerful and effective. Those who do not know about them or have not seen them in action do not realize how practical they are.

There are educators, psychologists and philosophers who set out to analyze the different steps and parts of thinking. They then attempt to teach these parts. This is a useless procedure. There is a huge difference between description and operating tools. A description is not the same as a usable tool.

Playing around with words is not sufficient. The tools mentioned here are based on an understanding of the brain as a self-organizing information system and the behavior of the neural networks in such a system. From that basis it is possible to design thinking tools that are practical and effective. Philosophical analysis can never do that.

Perception

As I have mentioned at many points in this book, perception is the key to human thinking. Very often nearly all the mistakes in thinking are mistakes of perception. Excellence of logic can never make up for mistakes of perception. By "mistake" I do not mean that something is "wrong," for inadequacy is just as dangerous as wrong.

True freedom demands breadth and flexibility of perception. You have to see widely. You have to see alternatives and possibilities.

In everyday real life, logic plays a minor role compared to perception. You see a situation in a certain way and the response is straightforward—you do not need complicated logical progressions.

In the Karee platinum mine in South Africa the members of the seven different tribes working there were always fighting. There were about two hundred and ten fights every month. Susan Mackie and colleagues set out to teach "thinking" to these totally illiterate miners who had never been to school for even one day in their lives. They taught thinking deep underground in the mines.

They taught a few of the CoRT tools for improving perception (to be discussed later). As a result the fights dropped from two hundred and ten a month to just four. Productivity was up.

It is important to note that this huge effect on behavior came about solely as a result of teaching "thinking." There was no attempt at all to change attitudes or behavior or to point out wrong behavior.

The Hungerford Guidance Centre in the UK takes youngsters who are too violent to be taught in normal schools. The principal, at that time, was David Lane. He started teaching the CoRT tools. The level of serious violence dropped from eight incidents a week to just one. Again, there was no direct effort to modify behavior—just the teaching of perception.

Classes of thirty twelve-year-old boys in Australia were asked if it would be a good idea if students were paid for going to school. All thirty of the youngsters thought it a very good idea.

Then one of the CoRT scanning tools was introduced. The boys used this tool in short discussion—about four minutes. As a result, twenty-nine out of the thirty had changed their minds. There was no argument. There was no attempt by the teacher to suggest considerations, just the perceptions scanning tool.

A teacher in New Zealand reported that teaching thinking to youngsters in prison reduced the rate of return to prison (recidivism) to one quarter of what it had been.

There is a club for the top women executives in Canada. I was once asked to address this club. I asked them to consider whether it would be a good idea for women to be paid fifteen percent more than men for doing the same job. Eighty-five percent of those present thought it a good idea—and about time too! I then asked them to use a simple scanning tool. As a result those in favor dropped from eighty-five percent to just fifteen percent. All of them were senior executives well used to thinking. So why change?

ATTENTION

PERCEPTION IS ALL ABOUT ATTENTION. What catches our attention? What inbuilt frames and prejudices direct our attention?

An explorer is sent to report on a newly discovered island. He reports back that there is a smoking volcano in one corner. There is also a strange bird-like creature that cannot fly. He is asked what else he saw. He reports that these were the things that caught his attention.

The explorer is sent back with explicit instructions to "look North and to note what you see" and then to "look East," etc. The explorer now "directs" his attention and sees much more than before; he comes back with a full report.

We have spatial directions like north, south, east and west. We have ways in which we can direct our sight. But what about directing our perception?

The CoRT program introduced perceptual directions as simple as north, south, east, and west.

Each direction was given an acronym. This is so the directions exist directly in the mind because they have a physical location there. Attitudes do not have locations.

So the simple PMI scan invites the thinker to look at the "Plus" (positive) points, then at the "Minus" (negative) points. And, finally, the thinker looks at the "Interesting" points. It was this simple scan that got twenty-nine out of thirty boys to completely change their minds about being paid for going to school.

Then there is the C&S which means looking at the "consequences and sequels." What are the immediate consequence; the short-term, the medium-term and the long-term consequences. It was this simple scanning tool that got the women senior executives to change their minds.

These tools are so simple that people claim to use them all the time. Every one of the senior executives would claim that she always thought of consequences. Yet being asked to do it deliberately and formally produced a huge change.

The OPV means looking at "Other People's Views." What is the thinking of the other people involved? It was this simple tool that changes behavior so dramatically in the Karee mine and the Hungerford Guidance Centre. The "tools" are so very simple that it is easy to see why educational theoreticians cannot see how they would work. But they do work—and very powerfully.

Try using the C&S on "what would happen if dogs could be taught to speak."

The tools simply direct attention. Instead of attention being directed by the situation or by established prejudices, there is a deliberate frame for directing attention. Logic will never change emotions. But perception will. If you see a situation differently your emotions change whether you like it or not.

A journalist once suggested that you could tell if your husband had a girlfriend by noting the length of his tie when he left after breakfast and noting the length when he returned in the evening. So one day the husband returns with a rather shorter tie and his wife gives him hell.

"Honey," he says, "I have been playing squash."

The emotions change immediately.

I once asked a group of six-year-old severe Down syndrome children to tell me the "Plus" points of a snake having a head at both ends.

They came up with many points including one point that stated if the snake went down a hole it could come out without having to turn around.

I gave the same exercise to five hundred top educators and secondary school children at a meeting in Belfast. None of them had that particular idea.

The tools are first practiced on fun and remote items. It is a bad mistake to practice the tools on "backyard" items. If you do that, the attention stays on the subject not on the "tool."

Fun and remote subjects are more interesting and the attention stays on the tool.

The biggest classroom I ever had was seven thousand four hundred children aged six to twelve years in a huge convention center in Christchurch, New Zealand, organized by Vicki Buck the mayor of that city. For ninety minutes, the youngsters enjoyed practicing these CoRT tools.

NEGLECTED

WE HAVE NEVER MADE AN ATTEMPT to change each perception explicitly. We can use examples. We can point out incorrect perceptions. We can seek to instill attitudes like "take a balanced view." None of these are anywhere near as powerful as the simple scanning tools of the CoRT program.

At the time of the Renaissance when the church established the software of thinking, there was no need to use perception because the "starting points" or perceptions were given by religious teaching. What was important to the church was logic and argument to prove heretics wrong. So this became the core of Western thinking. It is as important as the rear left wheel of a car: excellent but insufficient by itself.

We now know that perceptions can be taught. They can be taught in a simple, direct and powerful way. There is a great deal of experience with the CoRT program.

In business there is a modified version of the CoRT program called DATT (Direct Attention Thinking Tools). This is useful at all levels.

In the noisy mines of South Africa, hand signs were developed for the CoRT tools. You made the hand sign and both you and others responded to this. With Down syndrome youngsters, we also find hand signs useful. They make the hand sign (for example the sign for APC: Alternatives, Possibilities, Choice) and then respond to their own hand sign—so bypassing meta-cognitive problems in the brain itself.

THE SIX HATS, PARALLEL THINKING

IN ONE SCHOOL THE SIX HATS method is so widely used that the teachers use it in their own staff meetings as well as with the students. One day there was a visit by Government Inspectors. Conscious that the visitors did not know the parallel thinking method, the staff reverted to traditional argument. They reported that they found argument to be crude, primitive and ineffective.

There may be times when argument is the most appropriate way of exploring a matter. In general, however, argument is a poor way of exploring a subject. The wonder is that we have been satisfied with argument for so many centuries when it is such a poor thinking tool—such inferior human software.

The Six Hats method has been mentioned before in this book so there is no need to go into great detail. The Hats may be used in a sequence or even one at a time.

When Ron Barbaro was chief executive of Prudential Insurance, Canada, I saw him working with his executives. He would suggest an idea. They would immediately respond that it was impractical, too expensive, may be illegal, would not be accepted by agents, etc. He would listen and then say:

"That is excellent black hat thinking—now I would like the yellow hat, please."

The thinking would immediately switch to considering the possible benefits and the values and ways it could be done.

The sheer artificiality of the Hats makes a request for a change in thinking much more powerful than the usual exhortation, "to think more positively."

The Hats are used equally by four-year-olds in schools and by top executives around the world.

One chief executive told me that his six-year-old daughter was doing the Hats at school. Whenever he got angry with his daughter she would say:

"Dad, take off your Red Hat."

The colors of the Hat are:

WHITE: information, questions, what is needed, what is missing, how to get information.

RED: emotions, feeling, intuition with no need to justify or explain them.

BLACK: caution, careful, critical, risks, downside, potential problems.

YELLOW: benefits and values, the logical positive. How it can be done.

GREEN: creative, new ideas, possibilities, alternatives.

BLUE: the organizing Hat sets up the sequence, the outcome, what is to be done next. It decides the focus and what is to be achieved.

There are two very important points about the use of the Hats.

The first point is that the Hats are not judgments about people. They are directions in which to look, not characterizations of people. Everyone should be able to look in all directions. It is never a matter of saying: "She's Green Hat," or "He is Black Hat." This is a very important point because the temptation is great and psychologists love putting people into boxes.

The second point is also very important. At any one moment everyone is wearing the SAME Hat. This is what parallel thinking is all about. It is not about role playing and one person wearing one color hat and another wearing a different color. Parallel thinking means thinking in parallel. Everyone wears the same color Hat at any moment.

Deliberate Creativity Lateral Thinking

You cannot dig a hole in a different place by digging the same hole deeper.

Lateral thinking has to do with changing perceptions, concepts and ideas instead of working harder with the same ones.

Perhaps for the first time in history we can put creativity on a logical basis as the behavior of information in a self-organizing system.

In my book "The Mechanism of Mind," which was published in 1969, I suggested how the neural networks in the brain allowed incoming information to organize itself into patterns.

Patterning systems are necessarily asymmetric.

The path from "A" to "B" is not the same as the path from "B" to "A." This is the basis of both humor and creativity.

Any valuable creative idea will always be logical in hindsight. Otherwise we should never be able to appreciate its value.

Once the creative idea has been seen as "logical" in hindsight, then we say there was no need for creativity—all we needed was better logic in the first place.

It is because of this total failure to understand the nature of asymmetric systems that we have never understood creativity. Word playing philosophers could never understand the behavior of self-organizing systems which make asymmetric patterns.

So creativity was a mystical gift or a matter of special talent or even divine inspiration. Today we can see creativity as the logical behavior of information in a self-organizing system. There is no mystery.

I am referring here to idea creativity and change creativity. The English language does not distinguish between the two, which is why I had to invent the term "lateral thinking."

An artist may produce a work of art which is, of course, new and which has aesthetic value. So we call it creative. There may, however, be no element of change. The artist is working within his usual style, but applying the style to a new subject.

Some artists, especially in music, do use my work but I am essentially dealing with idea creativity and change creativity. This means creating new ideas and doing things in a different way.

Once we understand the basis of creativity we can design specific formal and deliberate tools. They can be very powerful.

I only intend to give two examples of such tools here. I have chosen the examples because they are very different from our normal thinking.

Provocation

Po cars have square wheels
Po planes land upside down
Po you die before you die
Po the factory is downstream of itself

Each of these statements is rubbish and contrary to normal experience. Ordinary thinking is about the "truth" and clearly these statements are not.

So there is a need to indicate that these statements are special: they are provocations. To indicate their special nature I invented the word "Po" (Provocative Operation). There is no indicator in ordinary language to indicate a provocation. The word "suppose" is much too weak.

With a provocation there may not be a reason for saying something until after it is said.

The provocation leads to new ideas.

Mathematicians are agreed that in self-organizing systems there is an absolute need for provocation. Otherwise the system settles down in a "local equilibrium." The provocation brings it nearer a global equilibrium. The process is sometimes called "annealing." This comes from making steel. The steel crystals lock in a position which might be stable but is not strong. So you reheat (provoke) the steel in order to allow the crystals to unlock and lock into a stronger configuration.

In a self-organizing system like the human brain, provocation is also needed.

It is clear that the need for provocation could never come from playing around with language, but only from an understanding of the underlying system.

MOVEMENT

ONCE WE HAVE PROVOCATION WE need a new mental operation called "movement." If we were to use our normal "judgment," each of the statements would have to be rejected as incorrect.

Movement is not just the absence of judgment. Movement is moving forward directly from the provocation to a new idea. There are several formal and deliberate ways of getting movement: extracting a concept; running something forward in time; imagining the behavior from moment to moment, etc. These are some of the ways of carrying out the mental operation of "movement."

From the "car with square wheels" we move on to the idea of "anticipatory suspension" where the suspension acts in anticipation of need.

From the plane landing upside down we get an interesting new aeronautic principle of a "reservoir" of lift which can be used when extra lift is needed urgently.

From "dying before you die" comes the idea of "living needs benefits" in life insurance.

From the "factory downstream of itself" comes legislation to ensure that a factory input on a river is always downstream of its own outlet and pollution.

There are ways of setting up provocations and ways of getting movement. There is no mystique about provocation.

Random Entry

This is a very simple and very effective technique of lateral thinking. Yet it is totally contrary to our normal logic.

In order to generate new ideas about a given focus you use a noun that is obtained at random from a list or the dictionary. There is no selection whatsoever.

Since the word is selected at random, any word would do for any focus. This seems like total nonsense in our ordinary thinking, but not in a patterning system.

Someone is living in a small town. On leaving home that person always takes the same main road to work and to go shopping. One day, on the outskirts of the town, the car breaks down and the person has to walk home. He asks around for the "shortest" way home. He finds himself getting home by a road he would never have used on leaving home.

If you start at the periphery you are bound by the pattern preferences that exist at the center. It is a perfectly logical process.

The random word "nose" used to generate ideas about an office copier leads to the suggestion of using "smell" as an indicator that the copier needs paper, toner, etc. It is easy to ignore flashing lights but difficult to ignore a bad smell. Action is immediate.

Tools

There is only a sample of the deliberate creative tools of lateral thinking. I have included them here to indicate that they are part of the new human software that is available.

Freedom and Creativity

It would be totally unrealistic to suppose that individuals need to be creative enough to generate unusual options as well as the more normal options, before choosing "freely" between them. If that were so there would never be real freedom.

It is enough to be able to think of the range of reasonable, uncreative options. There is no suggestion that you have to be creative to be free—unless you happen to be in prison.

CONCLUSION

THERE IS TYRANNY.

There is force.

There is coercion.

If there is no tyranny, no force, and no coercion, are you free?

The Christian Church puts a great deal of emphasis on "free-will." If there were no free will, then it would not be just to punish someone for doing something wrong.

The Law Courts take the same view. If someone is mentally incapacitated then that person may not know what he or she is doing. Of course, if the incapacity is caused by the person's own action—as in drinking to excess—then the full responsibility remains.

The Full Picture

If you do not have the full picture then you are not free to make choices or decisions. You may indeed feel free because there is no force or coercion which makes you do something. In practice, ignorance or limited thinking is worse than force because you are not aware of it. You may be fully aware of force, but you may be ignorant of your ignorance.

Just as a drunken person is legally responsible for the crimes committed under the influence of the alcohol, so a person who does not learn to think more broadly is responsible for the lack of freedom imposed on himself or herself.

In matters of education and schools, the State is guilty of not providing its citizens with the true freedom they deserve—the freedom to see options.

THE RUSH TO BE RIGHT

IN PRACTICAL TERMS, "TRUTH" IS important. We need to know that the clear fluid we are drinking is water and not weed killer. We need to know that the traffic light has indeed blocked traffic in the other direction at a crossroad.

The human mind wants "certainty." In early days we needed to be certain that the plant we were about to eat was indeed edible. We want to recognize situations as soon as possible so that we know exactly what to do about them. This is the very basis of our traditional thinking. Recognize a standard situation and provide the standard answer.

This intense "rush to be right" prevents exploration of the subject. That is why I mentioned "maybe" at the start of this book. "Maybe" opens up possibilities and alternatives. "Maybe" opens up different perceptions. "Maybe" slows down the rush to be right.

ARGUMENT

WE HAVE ALL BEEN BROUGHT UP ON the argument idiom.

So we take positions. If the positions are readily available and strongly labeled we welcome this. So we welcome labels like Democrat or Republican. Instead of having to figure out our own complex, we easily slide into the position made available for us.

It could be that in times past there were very different value systems between the two parties. This is probably not really the case today. The party labels are for the sake of administration and electioneering.

All parties try to do sensible things as determined by circumstance and expert advice.

Once we have a position, then we defend it vigorously. We also enjoy the opportunity of attacking the other position (or positions). This makes for an ease and vigor of thinking which we like.

At the same time, taking this position totally excludes exploration of the subject. Argument is a primitive, crude and ineffective way of "exploring" a subject. The wonder is that we have to put up with argument for so long.

This book has been about the importance of exploration. This means exploring the subject and opening up possibilities and options. Then we freely choose from this enlarged field.

DESIGN

WHAT FOLLOWS EXPLORATION?

We need to "design a way forward." This means constructive thinking, creative thinking and design thinking. This is very different from argument. These "design group" skills are very largely neglected in an education still fashioned by medieval theologians.

If you have only two possible parties to vote for, what difference does design make? You can design your voting habits. Instead of being consistent with family or personal tradition, you change your voting choices. When asked by opinion surveys, you choose always to reply "undecided" or "don't know."

Your actions become consciously designed and not unconsciously shaped by lack of exploratory thinking.

Better Thinking

I HAVE SOUGHT TO SHOW THAT thinking is not just a matter of intelligence. I have sought to show that there is more to human thinking than just recognizing standard situations and providing standard answers—excellent though this system may be.

I have sought to show that perception is a key part of human thinking. Perception determines everything else. Perception has been neglected by education.

I have sought to show that "human software" is available for enlarging the range and ability of human thinking. The "rush to be right" is not the only software available.

Possible

ALL THINGS SUGGESTED IN THIS book can be done.

There needs to be the will to do them. Defending existing idioms and habits is not the best way of making progress—no matter how skillfully this may be done. Critical intelligence is by no means the highest form of intelligence.

Critical thinking is like the brakes on a motor car. The brakes are essential to prevent crashes and collisions.

There is only one circumstance when you can drive on brakes alone. That is when the car is going downhill.

A society that overesteems critical thinking is going downhill.

There is a need for creative and constructive thinking to design the way forward.

APPENDIX

There is an established network of certified trainers around the world. They are capable of training courses in the Six Hats, Lateral Thinking, Simplicity and the Six Value Medals. Enquiries about training should be directed to "de Bono Thinking Systems."

de Bono Thinking Systems
2570 106th Street, Suite A
Des Moines, IA 50322
Phone: Toll Free: 1.877.334.2687 or
Direct: 1.515.334.2687
Fax: 1.515.278.2245
info@debonothinkingsystems.com
www.debonothinkingsystems.com

Representative bodies like democracies and the UN cannot easily have new ideas because their role is to represent current thinking—and a new idea is not current thinking. So putting forward a new idea is a high risk. For this reason I have set up a "World Council for New Thinking" to provide a focus and a platform for new ideas. Six Nobel Prize winners are joining me in this venture. See The World Council for New Thinking Web site.

JAICO PUBLISHING HOUSE

Elevate Your Life. Transform Your World.

ESTABLISHED IN 1946, Jaico Publishing House is home to world-transforming authors such as Sri Sri Paramahansa Yogananda, Osho, The Dalai Lama, Sri Sri Ravi Shankar, Sadhguru, Robin Sharma, Deepak Chopra, Jack Canfield, Eknath Easwaran, Devdutt Pattanaik, Khushwant Singh, John Maxwell, Brian Tracy and Stephen Hawking.

Our late founder Mr. Jaman Shah first established Jaico as a book distribution company. Sensing that independence was around the corner, he aptly named his company Jaico ('Jai' means victory in Hindi). In order to service the significant demand for affordable books in a developing nation, Mr. Shah initiated Jaico's own publications. Jaico was India's first publisher of paperback books in the English language.

While self-help, religion and philosophy, mind/body/spirit, and business titles form the cornerstone of our non-fiction list, we publish an exciting range of travel, current affairs, biography, and popular science books as well. Our renewed focus on popular fiction is evident in our new titles by a host of fresh young talent from India and abroad. Jaico's recently established Translations Division translates selected English content into nine regional languages.

In addition to being a publisher and distributor of its own titles, Jaico is a major national distributor of books of leading international and Indian publishers. With its headquarters in Mumbai, Jaico has branches and sales offices in Ahmedabad, Bangalore, Bhopal, Chennai, Delhi, Hyderabad, Kolkata and Lucknow.

SINCE 1946